ANCIENT CIVILIZATIONS

MESOPOTAMIA, EGYPT, AND THE INDUS VALLEY

ANCIENT HISTORY FOR KIDS
4TH GRADE CHILDREN'S ANCIENT HISTORY

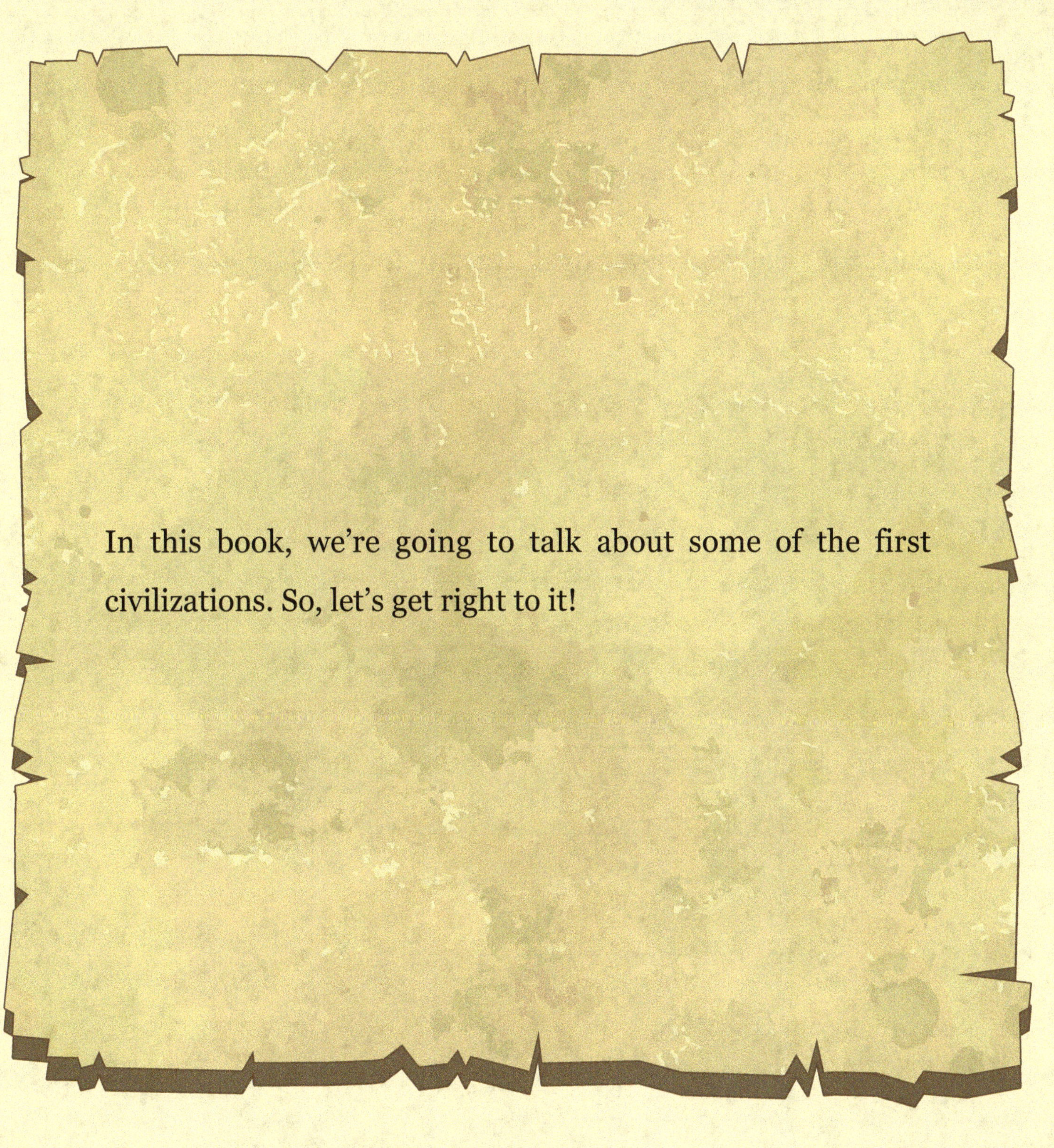

In this book, we're going to talk about some of the first civilizations. So, let's get right to it!

Rivers brought water, fertile land, and a means of transportation for ancient civilizations. For Mesopotamia, it was the Tigris and Euphrates Rivers. For Egypt, it was the Nile River, and for the Indus Valley civilization, it was the Indus River.

TIGRIS RIVER

MESOPOTAMIA

The land of Mesopotamia, which means "land between the rivers," got its name because it was wedged between two important rivers, the Tigris River and the Euphrates River. Primitive humans were nomads, which simply means that they moved from place to place to hunt and fish in areas where there were natural resources. Beginning about 10,000 years ago, people began to experiment with farming. Farming their own food meant they could stay in one place. The crescent of land between the two rivers had rich, fertile soil and it was an excellent location to begin the earliest ventures into agriculture. Today, this area is modern-day Iraq.

8000 BC

The first nomadic people gather in the "fertile crescent" area of Mesopotamia.

6000-7000 BC

People began to create pottery to store food and serve it. They experimented with different shapes and forms.

4500 BC

The civilization of Sumeria begins.

2500 BC
The civilization of Assyria begins.

1700 BC

The civilization of Babylonia begins. The first code of laws is created by Hammurabi.

LIFE IN MESOPOTAMIA

The northern part of Mesopotamia was covered with mountainous terrain and the southern portion was primarily marshlands and expansive, flat plains. The two rivers brought in fertile land for growing strong crops, which at that time were mostly wheat as well as barley. The two rivers made the transportation of goods easy throughout the area. Wool for cloth became an important export.

EUPHRATES RIVER

As the people began to grow more food, there was a change in the social structure. Slaves were the lowest class, but they were generally treated fairly. The common people were those who provided most of the labor along with help from slaves. Over 80% of these people were farmers. Closer to the top of the social classes were the merchants and craftsmen. During the Sumerian civilization, these classes created cuneiform writing in order to keep a record of imports and exports.

Higher ranking than the merchants and craftsmen were the soldiers who kept the civilization secure and conquered neighboring peoples. At this level, were also the educated scribes who were generally the sons of the elite class of nobles or priests. At the top of the social structure was the king and his right-hand manager who was called the vizier.

The Mesopotamian government was a combination of a democracy with a monarchy. The kings reigned over the people, who were organized into the four classes previously described—the priests and nobles, the upper class of scribes and the military, the lower class of laborers who were mostly farmers, and the lowest class, which consisted of slaves.

Religion was important to the Mesopotamians and their beliefs are some of the oldest that archaeologists have records to verify. They believed that their world was controlled by a group of gods and goddesses. They also believed that mythical creatures made everything in the natural world. Some of their major deities were Adad, Ashur, Enki, and Anu, but there were dozens of others. Their myths consisted of stories that were repeated and included demons with human bodies topped by animal heads and other monstrous creatures.

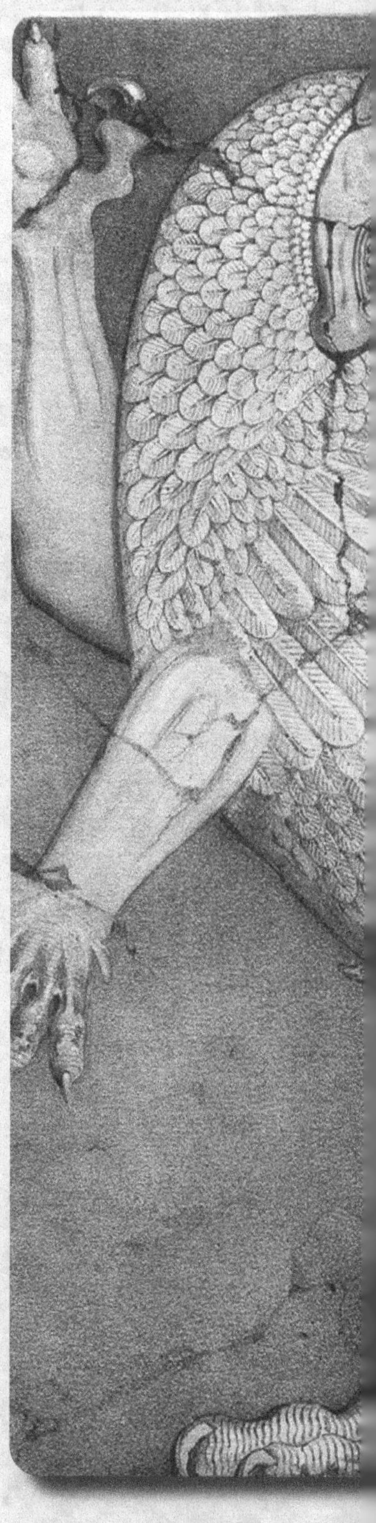

INNOVATIONS OF THE MESOPOTAMIAN CULTURE

This ancient culture developed the first system of writing. They are also credited with inventing the wheel. They learned to control both floods and drought conditions through the use of irrigation, which allowed them to become expert farmers.

EGYPT

There would have been no Egyptian civilization if it hadn't been for the Nile River.

Only 2 inches of rain falls annually in this desert region, but the river ensured fertile soil for crops. The river's delta is over 4,000 miles and empties into the Mediterranean Sea.

TIMELINE OF ANCIENT EGYPT

6000 BC

People begin coming to the Nile Valley to start settlements.

5000 BC

Egyptians have domestic sheep as well as cattle.

4500 BC

The Egyptians create sails for their ships so they can travel
faster on the Nile River.

3500 BC

Artisans and craftsmen paint the first walls with Egyptian writing, which is called hieroglyphics.

3000 BC

Villages are constructed in Egypt.

2500 BC

Construction begins on the Great Sphinx and Giza's Great Pyramid.

PYRAMID OF GIZA

1500 BC

The Egyptians stop building pyramids but continue to build many tombs in the location that became known as the Valley of Kings.

LIFE IN EGYPT

Over 90% of Egypt is a desert terrain. The Nile River flows from south to north and empties into a huge delta that connects to the Mediterranean Sea. The fertile land brought by the yearly flooding of the Nile River was where the Egyptians farmed.

The land is divided into four major regions:

NILE RIVER VALLEY
ARABIAN DESERT

LIBYAN DESERT
SINAI DESERT

The vast delta area is where most of the economy of the civilization took place. Farmers didn't own their own land because it belonged to their ruler, the Pharaoh. They were paid using a portion of the proceeds from their crops. One way the social structure in Egypt can be depicted is through the use of a pyramid. Slaves were the lowest tier and farmers had slightly more social standing than slaves. Craftsmen were considered more important than farmers. The Egyptian middle class consisted of soldiers and educated scribes. Religion was very important so the priests and nobles were almost at the top of the "pyramid." Almost at the very top was the vizier, who was the Pharaoh's most trusted government officer. There were other government officials as well, such as the chief treasurer and the public works minister. The king, known throughout Egypt as the Pharaoh, was at the very top of the pyramid.

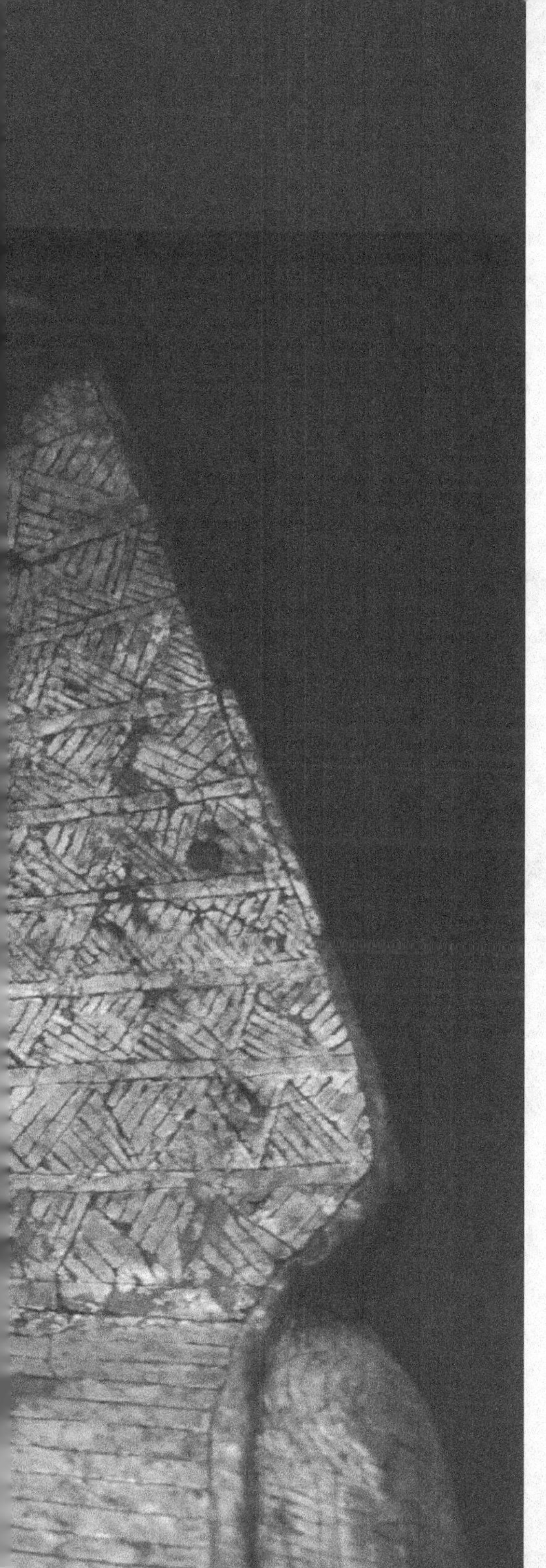

The Egyptians believed their Pharaoh to be like a god, so their government was a theocracy. He had complete power over the people and the kingdom. He did have trusted advisors, but he was still the final decision maker.

Religion was critical to the Egyptian culture. They believed in many different gods and goddesses. They had a strong belief in the afterlife. Many of the Egyptian deities had human bodies with heads of animals. They believed that the sun initially came out of an egg.

SOME OF THEIR MAJOR DEITIES WERE:

- Ra, who was the sun god and was depicted with a falcon's head
- Isis, who was the mother goddess
- Osiris, who was the god of those who had died and was in charge of the underworld
- Horus, who was the god of the sky
- Thoth, who was the god of knowledge

INNOVATIONS OF THE EGYPTIAN CULTURE

Even after the passage of thousands of years, the buildings that the Egyptians created are still standing. Their massive pyramids, temples, and other monuments are engraved with their hieroglyphics, which archaeologists have deciphered. The writings found tell their history and provide clues to these mysterious people.

INDUS VALLEY

The Indus River and its tributaries is one of the largest Asian river systems. Its terrain is primarily the Western Tibetan Plateau. The Harappans created a civilization along the river and their civilization was very successful from 2300 BC to 1700 BC.

TIMELINE OF INDUS VALLEY

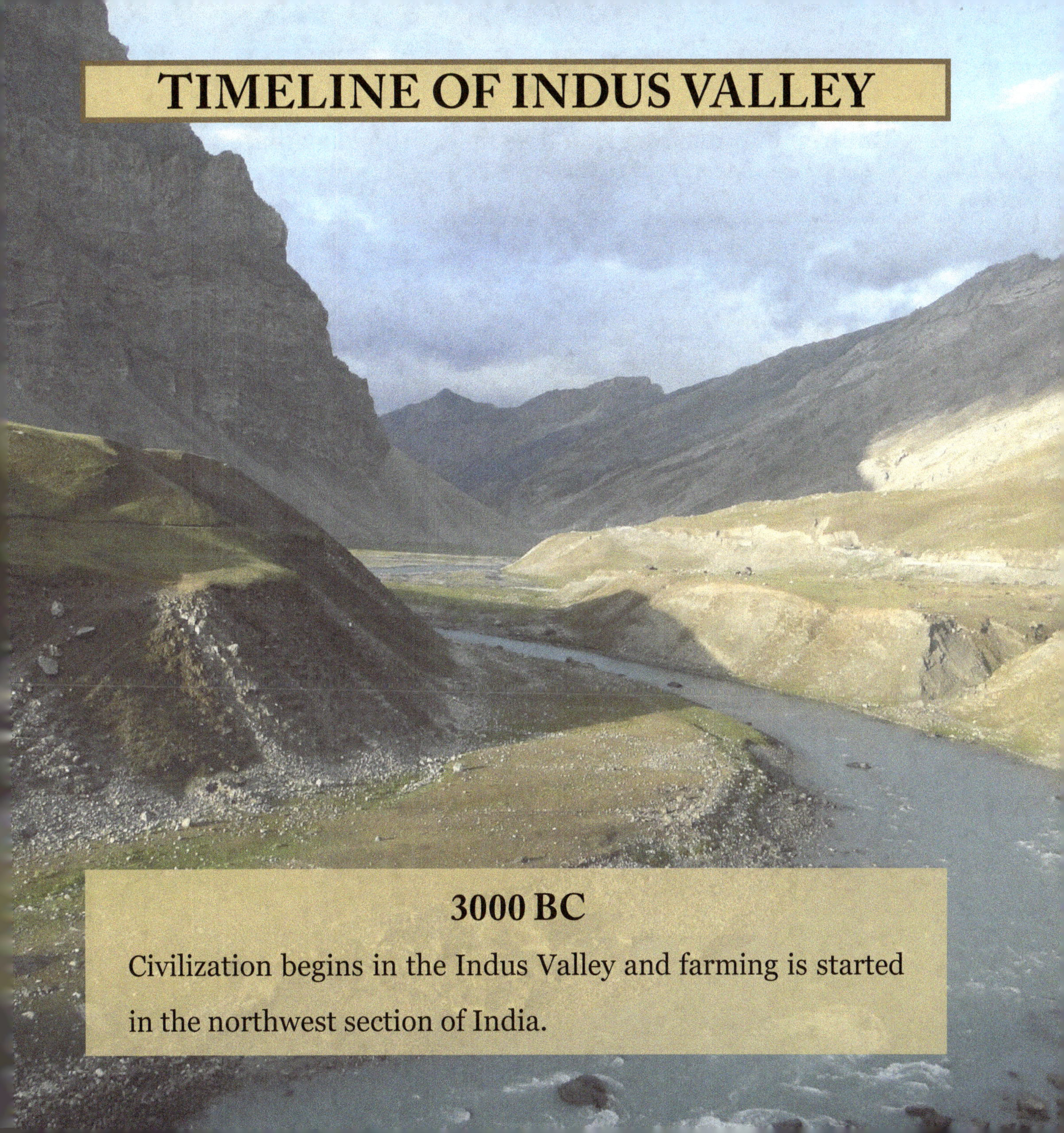

3000 BC

Civilization begins in the Indus Valley and farming is started in the northwest section of India.

2500 BC

Children in India are given toys made from clay that has been baked.

2400 BC

The golden age of the Indus civilization occurs during this time period.

INDUS VALLEY CIVILIZATION

1800 BC

The Indus Valley civilization goes into decline.

1500 BC

The Aryan people come into the area.

480 BC

The religion of Buddhism is begun.

LIFE IN THE INDUS VALLEY

The terrain around the Indus River had periods of drought as well as massive flooding from monsoons. It was challenging to farm there. As in Mesopotamia, wheat and barley were the major crops and the people also kept domesticated animals. Carts as well as boats were used for importing and exporting.

There was a strict social caste system in place there. Once you were born into a particular class there was no way to change your societal standing. Religion formed the governmental structure and order was kept due to strict religious beliefs and principles. From 1700 to 1100 BC, Hinduism was the dominant religion. Hindus believe in many different gods. Buddhism emerged as an important religion around 365 BC. Buddhism is based on the teachings of the Buddha.

INNOVATIONS OF THE INDUS VALLEY CULTURE

The Harappans created huge fortresses in each city for security. Walls were also built to manage the flow of trade and to ensure that settlements wouldn't be flooded. The Harappans also created the very first form of writing in India.

Primitive people were nomads until they began to farm and produce their own food. The innovation of farming allowed them to stay in one place and establish homes and communities. These ancient civilizations all started around prominent rivers. The earliest civilization, Mesopotamia, was begun in the fertile crescent between the Tigris River and the Euphrates River in what is the country of Iraq today. Over thousands of years, different groups of people created civilizations there.

The Nile River in Egypt was the site of another great civilization, the Egyptians. The Egyptians created their own language of hieroglyphics. They were expert mathematicians as well. They are probably best known for their many architectural marvels, such as the Great Pyramid at Giza. The Harappan civilization arose along the Indus River in India. Two major world religions, Hinduism and Buddhism, began there. Hinduism is the oldest world religion that is still practiced today.

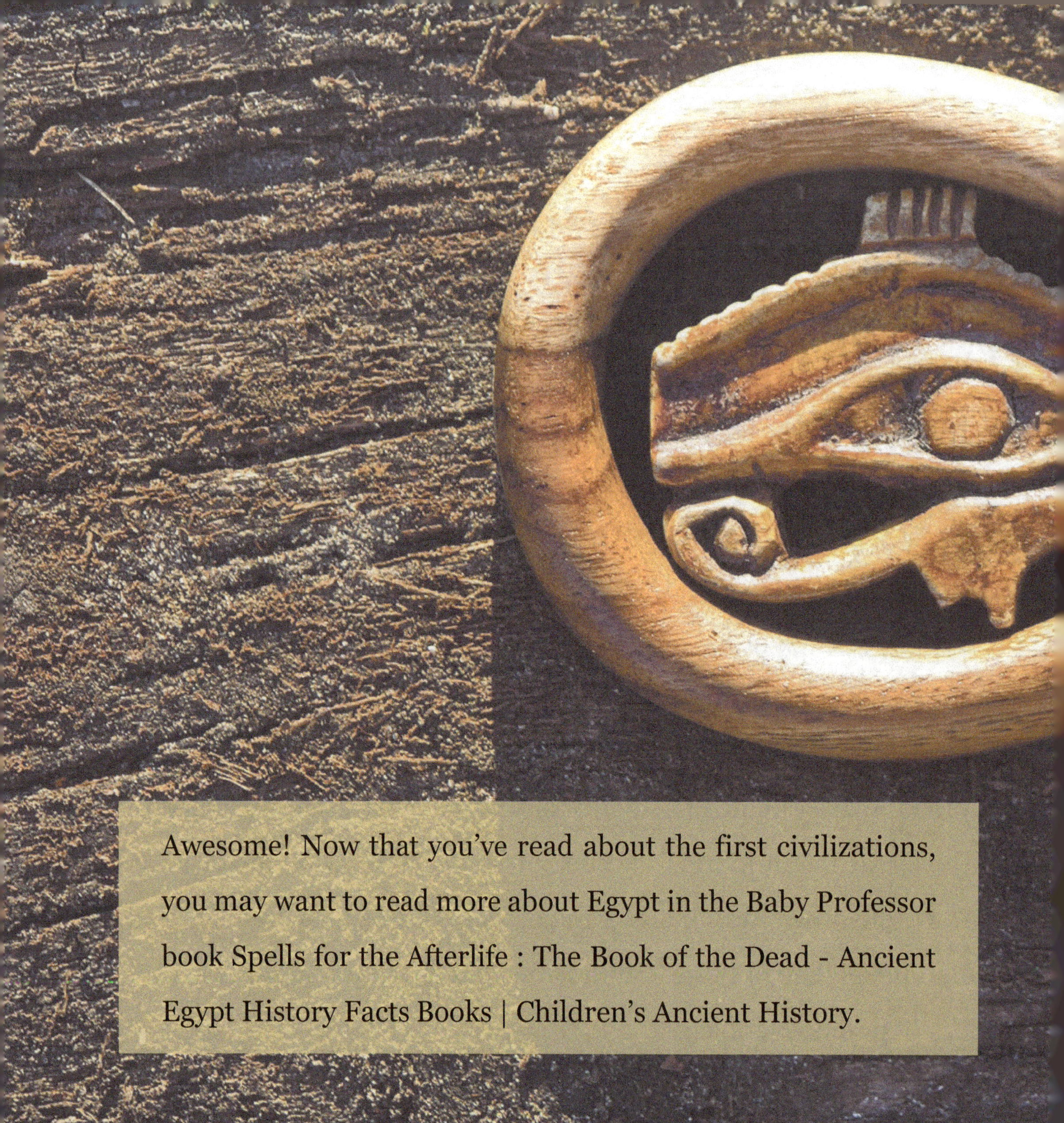

Awesome! Now that you've read about the first civilizations, you may want to read more about Egypt in the Baby Professor book Spells for the Afterlife : The Book of the Dead - Ancient Egypt History Facts Books | Children's Ancient History.

Visit
BABY PROFESSOR
EDUCATION KIDS
www.BabyProfessorBooks.com
to download Free Baby Professor eBooks
and view our catalog of new and exciting
Children's Books